LOST IN MY LABYRINTH

GAURI SHUKLA

ISBN 979-888569558-9

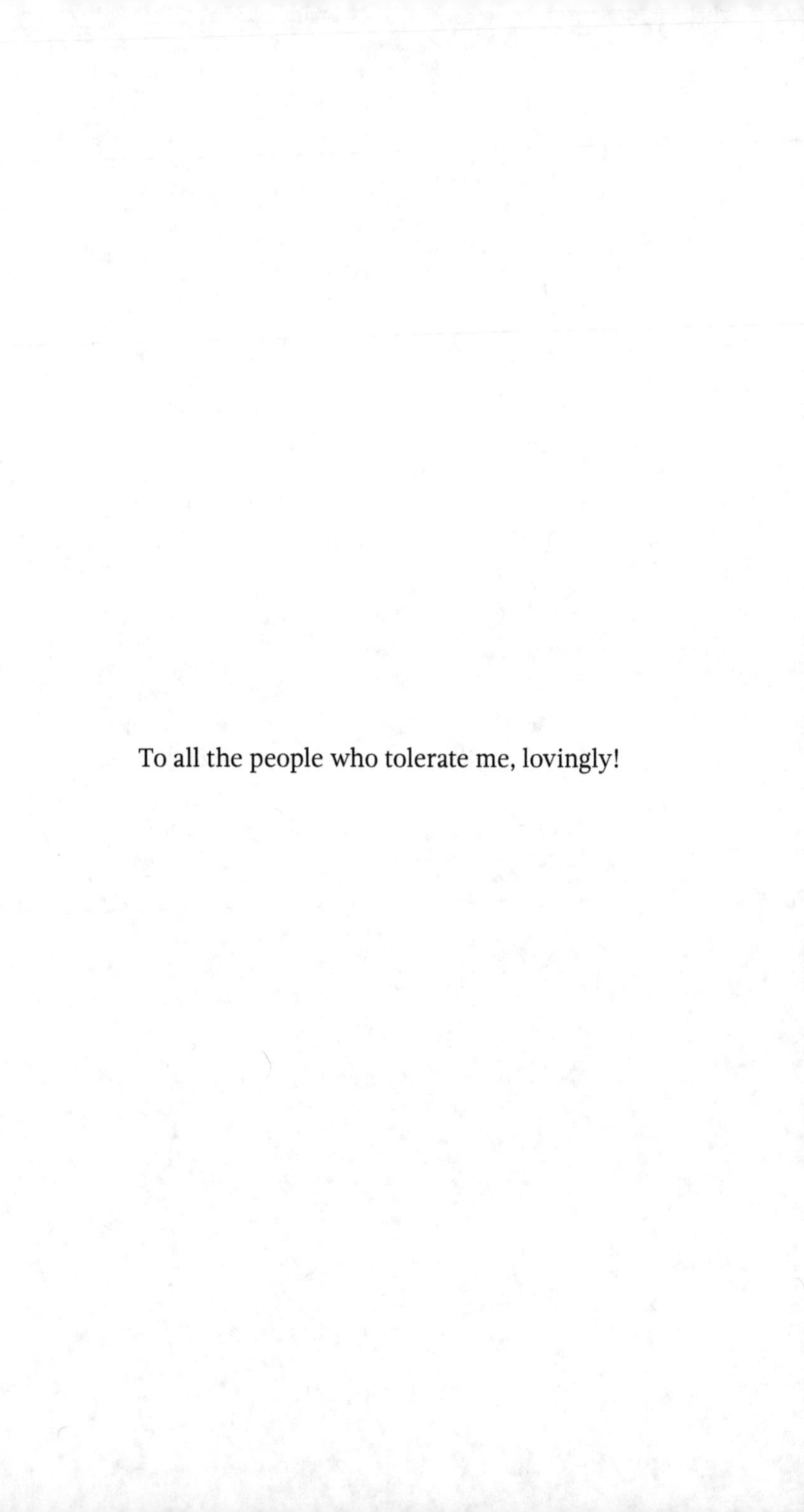

To all the people who tolerate me, lovingly!

Contents

Foreword

Gauri Shukla exhibits extraordinary talent voicing her thoughts through her words. The poetries are simple and yet they are very intricate to the one who reads them. Her writings beautifully capture the rogue sentimentality and the chaotic organisation. She masks her emotions behind the rhyming scheme of her verses. Her writings are not to be said to have developed from thought but to have been commemorated by her and be embodied in their true selves.

Where on one hand her writings in this collection could be represented through shades of black and grey, on the other hand, the feelings accumulated after reading Gauri's writings here have been cathartic. It brought all shades of blue, marking purgation, to me.

I met Gauri when I started the Academic and Creative Writing Training Internship program in mycompany (Nrityangana Kala Kendra) and she started working under my supervision as a trainee and then an intern. In the twelve weeks that we worked together, Gauri wrote some beautiful pieces; some of which have already been published. In fact, the book that you hold in your hands is the product of an individually assigned creative writing project that she worked on during the internship. She continues to work as a freelance writer for the company and keeps surprising me with her talents.

I can honestly say that I feel she has a really bright future and she is going to have many more gigantic achievements in her life. I am extremely proud of her for how far she has come and how much growth she has bestowed upon herself in the little time we had.

"Haunted" is an outburst in words of a suppressed shriek held in for long, being piled on ever since. Reading the poem you can actually feel as if someone was crying out loud but isn't expecting anyone to help her. We also witness an evolution, some restraint, some compromise, and an abundance of growth.

"Charged Guilty" is very humane and relatable. I, as a reader, could live through the character.

"I am a Tumultuous Poet" is the mirror of Gauri's soul which she presents bare to her readers.

The one sentence that I can put forward truthfully about "One True Sentence" is that 'it is a realistic walkthrough fantasy'.

"Lost in my Labyrinth" is an amazing start for Gauri Shukla and a treat for her readers. I'd highly recommend everyone to read this book and appreciate its nonchalance.

The illustrations have been beautifully done by Aishwarya Jayan, who has managed to capture the depth of Gauri's writings and mirror them.

Swarnika

Director
Nrityangana Kala Kendra

Acknowledgements

First of all, I would like to thank my mentor, Ms. Swarnika, who gave me this wonderful opportunity to put down my thoughts and feelings in the form of this book. To my parents and my brother, who have always had my back and supported me through every endeavor, I couldn't be more grateful.

This book couldn't have come together without the constant support and belief of some people that I love and respect a lot. I would like to take this opportunity to thank three of my seniors, Tushita A. Paul, Aiswarya Jayan, and Aprajita Khajuria who have always been a constant support system to me. Special thanks to Tushita A. Paul and Aiswarya Jayan, who played a very crucial role in getting this book ready; my friends, Ajay Nirmal, Tashneet Kaur, and Nishita Sharma, who have always believed in me more than I have myself.

Prologue

I wish there was a decoder in our my that could decode all my complex, apoplectic emotions. Sometimes, I just sit for hours trying to unknot the wires haphazardly snapping in my brain. Every so often, I am so close to a short circuit that I need to be very careful when fishing out the individual threads that somehow seem to have converged together. I look for inspiration in the air, desperate eyes scampering from the books on my shelf to the posters on my wall to the dirty pile of clothes hiked upon the couch; anything at all that might ignite the spark and refuel my empty tank of creativity. After a worthless tussle with my chaotic brain, I give up and go into the kitchen to look for food.

I sit back and sift through the folders in my cerebellum, on the lookout for something that will oil the rusty cogwheels of my imagination. Ah, found something! I throw the line with the bait and cautiously wait in curious exhilaration. A formless 'idea' taking shape before catching the bait. As the idea slowly takes shape and shade, still brewing, somebody slams the door of my room causing me to not only colossally flinch but also scaring the little idea in my head that was so close to its genesis. I am so stunned by the sudden intrusion that I don't even notice when my brother shoves in my face his phone to show me some meme he found too hilarious to not be shared. Aghast, I take the phone to look at that goddamned meme, which was, by the way, not hilarious at all. The next post though, as I scrolled, my dear friends, made me mull things over in my mind. It was something Ernest Hemingway said - "...sometimes when I was starting a new story and I could not get it going, I would stand and look out over the roofs of Paris and think, "Do not worry. You have always written before and you will write now. All you have to do is write one true sentence. Write the truest sentence you know."

This book contains four of my pieces that portray my feelings and thoughts that had accumulated inside my head over the past few months. The first piece titled 'Haunted' is a poem that talks about the vulnerabilities that each of us lives with. Sometimes, we hurt the people we love the most. If distancing ourselves from them helps to keep them safe, even if it hurts a lot, we do it. The second piece is a short story titled 'Charged Guilty'. Written in the form of a journal, it encapsulates the story of two girls in love but torn away by fate. The third piece is a poem titled 'I am a Tumultuous Poet'. The poem reveals the state of a poet's mind who wants to be better but is too tired to be because of all the drainage and exhaustion. The fourth piece, 'One True Sentence' is a letter to the readers from the author.

Writing makes me happy; my hummingbird pen deftly gliding across the whiteness of the pages, filling them with jostled words and inflammable feelings. The unremitting freedom that writing gives me will reverberate through the people who can find in my writing, a world that is alive and seething, with all the beautiful and the ugly, merged into one gargantuan world full of humanity. I feel elated as I put down the pen after my very last word, knowing deep inside that I have written something, for myself and for the people I love. And I hope they love this book as much as I love it - the first of many more to come.

CHAPTER ONE

HAUNTED

A forlorn castle and escapades
Explosions and heartbreaks
Faltering words and gasps of air
Choking hearts and flowing stray hair.

...

You are my castle
But I am going to explode;
When I do
I'll take everything down with me.

...

Everything inside me
Bubbling, rising, gasping for air,
Ready to gash out of my gaping wounds that only I can
see when I look at myself in the
mirror.

...

But I don't want to take you down with me
Those shreds and pieces will never become whole.
Like fire-parched paper, I will sway to the rhythm of
the wind.
All this hurt would disappear.

Trust me.
But do you trust me?

I have to leave the castle.
Do you hear the ticking of the time bomb inside me?
Tick tick tick tick
I know you hear it every time you lay your head on my
chest.
...
But do you feel it squeezing?
My thumping heart?
It has found a way of draining itself out.
It churns and churns for hours and then numbness.
...
I have to leave the castle
Before I detonate into a plume of smoke and
wretchedness.
...
I would no longer have to claw myself every night to
remind myself that I feel pain
I would no longer have to feel the pressing of the dam
of emotions and the frothing lake of
thoughts that I have carefully restrained in the chaos of
my mind.
...
Every inconspicuous incision on my emaciated body
creates a breach in that dam.
And when the walls break
I am going to drown.
My thwarting chest and tear-soaked eyes are just a
friendly reminder of the pain I like to sink
myself into.

Do you know you opened a chasm in my chest when
you first touched it?
Galloping through my veins
The chasm soundlessly keeps on expanding every time
you touch me.

...

There in the center of that silence is a loneliness so
profound,
The word itself has no meaning.
Devoured by loneliness, I know what it means now.

...

I remember tossing a coin into a wishing well.
When I turned away
A little boy kept it in his pocket.

I smile despite knowing my wishes belong to others.

I miss the people who hurt me
More than the ones who loved me back.
But I love you.
I'm saving you,
You see?
I don't want my castle broken.
...
I have been too sparing with the love I give
Because the love I got was abstract.
I had to write poetry filled with metaphors to guess
what it meant
And I'm still guessing...
And when I say I love you,
I mean you take up all the space in my brain not
crammed with chaos and pain and dying

and tears and the first thought I have every day.

When I don't say anything,
I am actually choking on everything I feel for you.
All this time, mostly,
I have been hurting in a singular sort of way
holding you
holding me
holding us, together
On my own
But falling apart on my own too
So, let me go
Before I explode.

CHAPTER TWO

CHARGED GUILTY

*"Feels like a river's rushing through my mind.
You're too good to be true.
How could I know one day I'd wake up feeling
more
But I had already reached the shore
Guess we were ships in the night, night, night.*
- V, Sweet Night"

Pride, greed, lust, envy, gluttony, wrath and sloth. The seven deadly sins. Pandora's curse. Mankind's despair. Can I add one more sin to the above-mentioned list of cardinal sins? Can I add 'guilt' to the list? Guilt when instead of becoming a source for penance, becomes a source of self-destruction, is a sin.

9th December

My name is Hestia and I'm twenty-one years old. I suffer from 'survivor's guilt', one of the many symptoms of post-traumatic stress disorder. I don't know if there's a term to describe how I feel but I definitely do not want to live and yes, I believe, I strongly believe that I should've been the one to die, instead of her. I don't exactly know why I'm documenting this, whatever this is, but it's important. The lines of her face are slowly blurring and mixing into a myriad of different colours that I don't recognise. Her beautifully sculpted jaw, her electric blue eyes, wavy dark brown curls settling carelessly on her forehead, shadowing the depth of those eyes that were capable of reading anything and anyone. I need to remember all these details. They cannot be fading and mixing into some soddy glunk of mismatched images in the infinite chaos of my brain. And since I'm free anyway, with nothing else to do than look back at the past and devise plans to somehow punish myself for my sins, I shall go ahead and rewrite her, remould her in the way I remember; singe her memories in the ridges of my brain such that they become inseparable. The pain, the remembering, after all, keeps me sane.

11th December

It's true how sometimes we get to know a person better in death. They leave a trail behind for us to follow; a scent that proves they existed. They leave their fingerprints on inanimate objects and animate objects alike. I can still feel the burning sensation of her hands on my back. I can feel the butterflies fluttering as I recall the slight brush of our fingers as we walked down the town street. I remember the way her fingers suddenly retracted after the slight touch and folded as she slid her now sweaty palms into the pocket of her blue ripped jeans. For some damned reason, she always wore ripped jeans. I remember asking her if she did not have anything else to wear! "I like them", she replied with a soft smile. Okay. "What else do you like?" She looked at me with doe eyes that would send me reeling into another dimension. "I like to remake things."

12th December

The first time I met her, she was holding a torn, wretched-looking leaf in one hand and a skateboard in another. I like to think it was fate that made us cross paths. The idea of 'fate' makes everything more cryptic. It was a windy autumn evening. The sun had slowly lulled itself to sleep leaving a reddish-orange afterglow in the sky. The leaves were slightly quivering in the wind and the smell of freshly made coffee whiffed from one of the windows on the street like a little plume of invisible cloud and settled on my nose. I saw her across the road fiddling with her skateboard while picking up crushed, trodden leaves. She collected them all as I watched her from a distance. She then, very carefully, placed them in a folder that she was carrying. Suddenly, she looked up in my direction, stared for like five seconds, gave a smile and went back to work. I remember how my heartbeat had stopped in that one moment when she looked at me, just like a criminal that's caught in the middle of executing the crime. Her smile felt like a gentle, cold stream running over the scorched earth of my soul.

13th December

The room smells stale. The walls are of an off-white biscuit colour that reminds me of the sanatorium very much. I don't like it. I feel like a hostage in this room. I cannot let ma know about this. She's already worried about our expenses after settling in a new place. The doctors suggested "a change of scenery". I am not very sure if the change of scenery is helping much. How do I tell ma that no matter where I go, I'm going to carry the war inside me everywhere? We're one. Like cancer, it has metastasized and formed its own colony of blood vessels and blood supply. It's living inside me and thriving off me and I don't know how I can separate it from me without tearing myself apart.

The night, I am specifically scared of the night. It brings with itself unwanted memories that hunt me down and hold the capacity to shred me to pieces. Memories are like wolves. You cannot lock them away and hope they never find you out or leave you alone. At night, the darkness seems to seep into my soul through the skin and settle there, like a heavy boulder that won't roll off. I lay still, unmoving, scared of disturbing it lest it stays there forever. Every night, I see it happen, the dark formless phantom glides into the room through the window in or the space beneath the door or the space behind the cupboard or from under the bed, and floats directly above my body. It then slowly lands itself upon me and percolates like rain into my bones. I have never dared to get up once it has settled itself inside me but I really believe that if someone was to look at me, they'd notice my body a few hues darker than it is.

15th December

That time when we lay down staring at the stars on the hood of that broken down car on the knoll, she asked me what I wanted to do when I grew up. I said I wanted to learn all the instruments present in the world. She let out a soft chuckle and looked at me with those deep blue eyes that gleamed under the stars. I saw swirling pools of turquoise in her eyes when she was completely ignorant about it.

I should've kissed her then. I know I wanted to. What kills me is that I know she wanted to as well. I live with incomplete feelings. Feelings that could never find a release and then she dissipated into thin air. And now, I'm a demon, living in a labyrinth of self erected walls that save me from the world and the world from me. It's amazing how we humans are capable of feeling things. This little heart of ours that keeps pumping life into the dead nooks of our body is the reason behind our breaths. And what is death but the distance between two breaths. Stretch the distance between those two fateful breaths, and you are standing on the threshold of death. And you look back and see your loved ones, standing there, crumbling in pain, dried up and brittle like pieces of chalk, while you stand there helplessly, unable to do anything, anything at all that will lessen the pain or make things alright. No amount of clawing and screaming and running and begging will bring you back. You're nothing but a mirage, a reflection of the past with no present or future. Like a soul aimlessly stuck in the invisible space between stifling dimensions. No sense of belonging but a heart that clenches at the thought of home. No home but a heart that aches for the warmth of hugs and the comfortable tinkling laughter of the people you love. Death is scary. But what if it's peaceful? Is it? She would know.

16*th* December

In the sanatorium, the people dressed in white laboratory coats would walk into my room and ask me every day what I was looking forward to. And each day, to everyone's dismay, I'd say, "Death." A lost case was what they labelled me as. I was lost. I am lost without her. They asked me to release the pain, the guilt, the tears. I don't know-how. The tears don't come. After her death, the first few days was the only time I was alive. I've been dead ever since. I've been haunted by her memories every day since the moment she left. The memory of that fatal day washes over my haggard mind in a flash, faster than lightning. It goes as fast as it comes, not giving the brain any time to even process the image. And the brain is back to being its sloth self, ambushed in a trap.

17th December

The first time she called me by my name, goosebumps rose all over my skin. Hestia. It would roll off her tongue so easily. My name had never sounded so enchanting before. The last time she took my name, I had stood in front of her, with strength bleeding out of my arms, helpless, as the darkness engulfed us. Imagine loving a ghost. I am in love with her memories and those memories have now become my reality. Her room used to smell like her. An old bookshelf with books from authors I had never heard of. She read so much poetry that everywhere you looked, there was some piece of paper stuck with scribbles on it. Potted plants adorned her window sill and a book lay plopped on the footrest beside her bed with a bookmark that she had made. A half-eaten doughnut lay on the bedside table. A few of her clothes lay scrunched up on her bed. Posters of rookie bands and a few polaroid shots stuck to the light brown walls of her room above the bed. I imagined her lying on her bed, head on the edge, book in one hand and the doughnut in the other. Eyes hardly visible through those dark brown curls that made her face look so mysterious and elysian at the same time. And so, sitting in the room with her memories, I conjured her up, my mythical creature. As a pause amid the hum of my thoughts, as a blank in the pictures of the past, as a dark spot amid my feelings, I was capable of conjuring all kinds of gaps. And when I was not thinking of her, the vacancy in my head was like the space left by a newly pulled tooth still conscious of the pain and rot that had once filled it.

18th December

We cannot decide to love. We cannot compel anyone to love us. There's no secret recipe, only love itself. And we are at its mercy –there's nothing we can do. As I look out the window at the pale cheerless yellow of the sun,

I am reminded of the tree-lined streets and I see her skateboarding down the streets, curls dancing in the air, hands out for balancing, wondrous electricity in the blue whirlpools of her eyes. She loved that skateboard and the freedom it gave her as she flew through the autumn drenched streets with no care in the world. I still have it with me. That was the only belonging of Celeste that I brought with me to my new hell hole. I have plans with that skateboard.

20th December

I remember that day too vividly. The light-drenched sky, the calls of the cicadas from the hundred-year-old trees, the winds wrestling over every almond leaf. The golden quivering and sparkling of the air when the sun goes down and turns the streets and their perching houses shades of pink and honey. Despite the slight chill in the air, the heat was like a fever. She looked ethereal against the setting sun. Her edges etched in reddish light, like the entrance to a place on fire. Celeste was teaching me to skateboard. I felt the hairs on my handstand as she held my arm and guided me to balance myself on the skateboard. I had never known this feeling before. It washed over me like a wave, suffocating and relieving at the same time. She would then look at me with those eyes and I would lose myself in their invisible blue currents that took me places. Those eyes haunt me. Everyday. Because when she jumped in front of that speeding car to save me, the last things I remember are- her luminescent blue eyes that had faded into a dull dead colour and my name on her tongue. Hestia.

I have been inadequately punished by Celeste as she forced me to live in a world without her. But how do I punish myself? I charged myself 'guilty' the moment she died for me. I'll take her skateboard, the very means that took my Celeste away and I'll follow her into the dark labyrinth. She won't be here to save me this time, after all. This is it. This is a fair and final judgement.

CHAPTER THREE

I AM A TUMULTUOUS POET

I am a tumultuous poet
Lost in my labyrinth
Finding poetry in cut-down trees
And trodden leaves
In torn, half-burnt letters
And lovers turned traitors
In unfinished song lyrics
And quaint Athenian panegyrics
...
A raging battlefield on two legs
In combat with itself
Picking up my calloused dregs
I place them on the mantel shelf
Hurting no one but myself

I want to be better
But I am too tired to be
In want of just a shelter
From all the agony

...

No, I am not broken
Just a little exhausted
Fractured and forsaken
Maybe, a little frosted?

...

A tear turns into a waterfall
As the breach in the dam deepens
The lake of emotions floods, speeding down the knoll
Into the garden of Eden

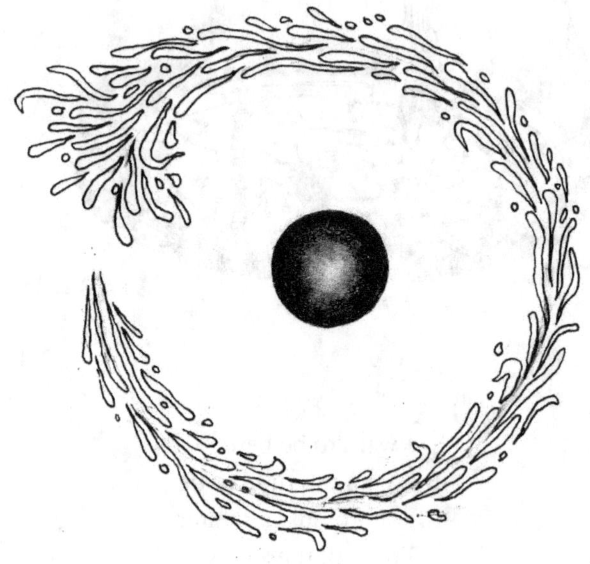

Like the brightest star in the sky
I shall burn for a hundred million years
Before I decay into myself.
I shall then birth a new star, a new life.

An ending and a new beginning-
And it'll all belong to me.
I am the black hole
And the galaxy that revolves around it
I am the island
And the ocean that surrounds it
I am a child of this mother Earth
And an unsung poet
Whose ballads will soon make rounds about it.

...

CHAPTER FOUR

ONE TRUE SENTENCE

What's the truest sentence I know? Everything that goes around, comes around. The great truth; the crux of the universe! Everything that goes around, comes around. We'll ponder moreover this statement later. Right now, I want to talk about my favourite space book. I was eight when my father got me a space book. He could've gotten me a beautiful vintage hardcover of Grimm's Fairy Tales but instead, he went for a space book. Not that I'm complaining but I would've really appreciated a vintage hardcover of Grimm's Fairy Tales or maybe Hans Andersen's Complete Fairy Tales! I do not know my fairy tales! Anyways, the space book was enough to stop me from nosing around in other people's businesses. Day and night, I would have my head buried in that book until it was confiscated by my lovely mother, owing to my resistance to sleeping. At night, in the ghostly darkness of the room, all those pictures from the book would come alive in my brain like figments of a rich imagination. They would illuminate into a thousand sparkling stars and cloudy nebulae, across my inward eye. I'd see the frosty diaphanous rings of

Saturn; I'd dodge the shapeless, amorphous asteroids in the asteroid belt, floating between the orbits of Mars and Jupiter; I would try to reach the moon and make sure to leave my handprints and footprints, along with my name, on the surface of the moon so that everybody who ever landed on the moon, knows a certain Gauri Shukla.

I still remember some of the dreams I had back then because they were just so weird and so awesome. I swear to God, if I ever wrote a script and presented it to Marvel Studios or Christopher Nolan, they'd be tempted! I had the entire interstellar space and multiverse thing going on in my mind long before they dropped the aliens and the Avengers. I would tell my parents and friends very passionately about these dreams and they'd laugh or give me an amused grin which only meant, "Oh look! Our kid is so adorable having such ludicrous dreams!" That was how I was brushed off and my luminous dreams, along with me. But, here comes the kick in the gut for me- as I stepped into the race of being the best, the most extraordinary, the favourite, the smartest kid who makes her parents and teachers proud, I let go of the things that made me happy. Lost in the practicality of life, I tried to find happiness in other things, like school, homework, extra-curricular activities. And while all these things shaped me and my childhood, when I look back, I regret letting go of things that made my soul burn with a passion so feral that sleep was a hindrance. I wanted to learn classical dance, took classes too but left later on. I began with keyboard lessons too but left them also because I had to study. BECAUSE I HAD TO STUDY? Might appear as an extremely lame excuse. And yes, I was also perhaps being lazy. But, I was also not sleeping till three in the morning because I had to get the highest marks in the class. I'd go through the concepts over and over again, living with the fear of having missed something. At one point, my parents got worried about my health because their daughter was studying for eight hours straight without food and water. I could have just gone to the Himalayas and meditated on one foot! The frenzy that had taken over me would have at least subsided then.

It wasn't that I didn't enjoy studying. I actually loved it. My favourite subjects were English, Biology, and Chemistry. But I wasn't just studying because I enjoyed the process, it was also for the marks, for the praise, and for the pride. And I studied with strenuous focus. Alas! It was this very focus of mine that lured my parents and myself into the 'great damned pit.' And also, there was this one pandit[1] who had looked at me and exclaimed emphatically to my parents, "She'll build a hospital in your name." Now, two things - first, I am never going to forgive the man; second, his statement had a loophole that my overly excited parents kind of overlooked. I don't really have to be a doctor to build a hospital and name it after my parents. But a ninety-seven percent in the board examinations and the preposterous prophecy of the all-knowing saint was enough to make me land with Science in class eleven. And then, like every Science student in the country, I was to choose a coaching center and begin my entrance preparations. So, I slogged for six hours in school first and then six hours in the coaching, every day of the week with zero time for self-study. I wanted to read Kafka, Shelley, and Plath; instead, I was trying to cram the chemical composition of benzophenone.

In the fall of 2019, I began with my undergraduate degree in English Honours. Surprise! After working my fingers to the bone for two years in Science, I was pursuing Humanities. My parents had realised long back that I didn't want to continue with science in the future and they had no choice but to support me in whatever I wanted to do. Sure, my mother had her sudden bursts of indignation at times but she would always manage to trust me in the end which is something I am immensely grateful for. College changed me. I went from a shy, reticent girl to a person who isn't scared of standing her ground and fighting for what's right. Things that I had only read about in history books like the idea of 'feminism' and the 'caste system' became topics that affected me greatly. I remember our teachers used to tell us in school that once out of this safe haven, the world will open up like an ocean full of precious jewels and deathly sea monsters, full of darkness and light, mysteries and memories, opportunities and heartbreaks.

When I was in school, we were once asked to fill out some forms which required us to fill in our categories. I was a little confused about something in the form and asked my classmate to show me how he did it. I saw the hesitation flash across his face before he showed me his form. He had tick marked the box belonging to the non-general category. That was the first time I realised that in our country, the word 'caste' evokes various sentiments and my classmate was worried he'd be looked down on or seen differently because of that. The slight flinch of his fingers clutching the paper and the reluctance on his face hurt me in an acute way. The next incident took place in college when a group of girls very nonchalantly remarked how seats were being given to less-deserving people. And I saw my friend (she did not belong to the general category) standing there motionless, looking at her feet, saying nothing. How difficult is it to treat someone with kindness? How difficult is it to make someone smile? How difficult is it to treat the other person with respect? It was us, humans who created these walls between people and drew fences and lines to demarcate countries and rule them. We were all born as equals. What happened? When our mode of origin is the same and our mode of decay is the same, then why do we live so divided, so full of hate and anguish?

If the world wasn't already ailing, the Covid-19 pandemic definitely knocked the remaining strength out of it. I won't go into the details of Covid's machinations, but I miss college and I miss sitting in classrooms with my friends. I miss our early morning banters and I miss sitting in the sun reading a book or hogging food in the canteen. Three years of college life, gone. I don't want to dwell upon the things I've missed and I try really hard to not let it get to me but sometimes it hits me like a speeding truck and I spiral down into the rabbit hole. Only, I don't find adventure down there.

On days I lose hope and tumble down the dark tunnel of despair, I repeat to myself my father's words, "You don't see it now but all the pieces are falling together in place. You think it's the end but this is just your grand design coming together into one whole colossal piece. Be patient and persevere. Riding life is not for the faint of hearts, have courage and believe in yourself, it'll be the most adventurous ride you ever take." Life does go on, no matter what. As crippling as the ride may get, we don't have the option to jump off the wagon. So, we keep at it. We take one step at a time and we continue till we begin to walk straight again. We relearn to live and we keep at it until we make things seem a little normal again. And in this journey of life that I've undertaken, I wish to be a good human being that lives in the world, not just endures it, not just suffers it, not just passes through it, but lives in it. I want to be able to look at the world, live recklessly, take my chances, make my own work, and take pride in it. The rest shall be taken care of for everything that goes around, comes around.

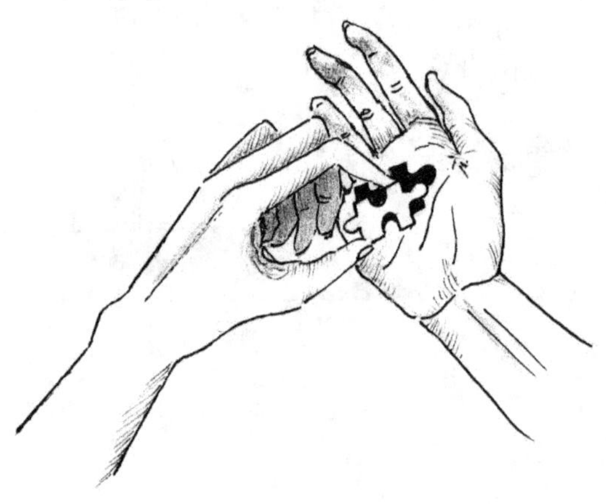

Gauri Shukla

Gauri Shukla is a third-year Literature student pursuing her passion for reading and writing from the University of Delhi. President of the Literary Society of the college, she is an avid reader who yearns to get lost in estranged, galvanic worlds of art. A national-level debater, she is someone who doesn't shy away from speaking her mind. An ardent scripturient, she has written articles for The Times of India, The Hindu, The Redstockings Chronicles, etc. She's currently working on a South-Asian anthology as an editor alongside editors from Bangladesh and Pakistan. Her main interests of study lie in Diasporic postcolonial and African-American literature. She wishes to document experiences and sentiments of different people, belonging to different cultures, all around the world and establish herself as a writer that connects with her readers. She believes life is too short and time is fleeting thus, each moment needs to be savoured and felt to its optimum level. She likes to describe herself as a wandering cloud that romances with the sky, lost yet free.

Book Reviews

- Dr. Mukti Sanyal (Former Principal of Bharati College, University of Delhi) - Beautiful, cryptic outpourings of a sensitive GenZ on dealing with self erected walls; a robust first time for a book.

- Dr. Sonali Jain (Professor, Bharati College, University of Delhi) - Insightful, compelling and vulnerable.

- Dr. Anoop Bhogal-Nair (Senior Lecturer in Marketing & Consumption, Leicester Castle Business School, De Montfort University) - Unapologetic, emotive, personal, and deeply curious. Gauri's words transport the reader into the crevices of human emotion. A truly passionate portrait of human vulnerabilities.

- Saba Shekh (Student of Masters in English Literature, Jamia Millia Islamia) - Gauri is blessed with a glorious gift of talent and her work is always a joy to read. Impeccable work.

- Tushita A. Paul (Masters of Commerce, Narsee Monjee College of Commerce & Economics) - A refreshing take on pain and life.